THEY CAME WITH WINGS, WHISPERS AND FUR

Miriam Caudillo

Introduction

The One Who Walks with Wings, Numbers, and Whispers

The first sound is silence, yet it trembles like a hidden song waiting to be heard. In that silence, a call rises, ancient and undeniable, reaching for every heart that has ever longed to be whole. It is not shouted across the mountains or carved into stone, but carried softly through the spaces between this world and the next. There, a woman walks. Her steps do not fade; they echo across time.

Miriam is her name. She is not just a traveler of paths, but a keeper of remembrance, a listener of truths whispered by Spirit, a healer whose presence stirs the unseen. She was born under the sacred vibration of Master Number 33, guided by compassion, divine wisdom, and a mission that stretches beyond our own realm and into the next. Encoded with the blueprint of service and spiritual mastery, her soul vibrates with a frequency that heals and calls all who listen to understand the wisdom and hope she shares.

Miriam isn't walking this spiritual path alone. Throughout her journey, she is accompanied by sentient messengers from the animal kingdom who speak to her in their own unique way, in signs, feathers, fur, and sometimes caws, and with the silent knowing we can all share if we listen.

To Miriam, Mocha, her small white dog, is her companion and her spirit animal. More than a friend, she's a guardian, an empath, and a soul mirror that reflects Miriam's light like no other. Softening the world's edges with every step of her paw, she is a reminder of the sacredness of simple presence.

Yet Mocha is not the only one to walk beside her. The journey is shared with crows, winged sentinels of shadow and truth, delivering messages from the unseen. They embody wisdom, intelligence, transformation, and good fortune, and in many Native traditions, they are honored as messengers between realms.

Hawks circle above her path, sharp-eyed and watchful. A dove glides close, carrying the remembrance of love that never dies. Butterflies drift softly in her wake, emissaries of souls and bearers of hope, joy, and change.

Each of these beings helps Miriam to chart her course through dreams and daylight, serving as her council of companions and a living testament, calling forth through her communion with the living world the life that exists beyond.

If you've chosen this book, or if it has chosen you, within it, you'll bear witness to Miriam's awakening, and summon your own. It is a portal, a threshold between realms. Let the numbers align, let the winds speak, let the creatures gather, and step forward into a sanctuary created by Spirit, holding space for the journey that is yours.

Table of Contents

Chapter 1

The Visitor Above the Sunroof

The first awakening came one early morning, when the light was soft and the streets were quiet. Miriam's sweet companion Mocha had only recently entered her life; a small canine guardian wrapped in white fur.

On a morning walk with Mocha, Miriam felt a hush in the air, a slightly unfamiliar stillness, as if something (a soul or a shadow) had paused just long enough to let her notice. In her car, after safely buckling little Mocha into her seat, Miriam heard a sound that wasn't coming from the radio or from any passerby.

Tap. Tap.

It was coming from above.

She slid the sunroof visor open and looked up to see a single crow perched on the roof of her car, its piercing eyes blazing through glossy black feathers, staring directly at her.

He cawed once, loud and clear, a message. And the world fell still again, for a single breath at least. Miriam turned to Mocha and whispered, "We have a visitor."

And something inside Miriam stirred, even as she smiled at her little dog. It was a memory long buried, a connection deep within the soul, and too old even for language. Miriam felt seen.

At home, under the warm glow of the lamp on her desk, Miriam searched the internet for the meaning behind a visit from a crow. It wasn't simple curiosity or a passing interest in nature that drew her to search. Each word she read felt like a key turning in an ancient lock, as if she were not learning something new but uncovering what her soul had always known. In that moment, the act of searching became an act of remembering.

What she found opened a door in her heart, her mind, and her soul. She read that crows were:

- Messengers.
- Protectors.
- Guides from the beyond.
- Carriers of transformation.

The veil that had obscured the past, that separated the present world from the eternal, thinned. Her heart raced with possibilities and joy. She had received an invitation.

And so, here is yours:

It was never just a walk.

It was never just a bird.

It was the day the sky whispered back.

The journey began with one crow… and two awakened hearts.

Chapter 2

The Ritual Before the Wings

Long before the crow tapped the sunroof…

Long before Mocha padded beside her, quietly knowing… Long before her eyes trained on telephone poles and skies…

Miriam was just a woman in a shop, holding a plaque with simple words that drew her heart.

Miriam didn't know she was witnessing a ritual. It didn't look like one, after all. Yet it evoked curiosity, inspiration, something gentle, like the sound of a faint bell in the distance.

It was a small wooden plaque inscribed with the words:

"Home is where your heart is."

Something tender stirred in her. She wanted those words not only on her wall but woven into her life. So she purchased it, brought it home, and hung it above her living room window. Beside it, she placed a small sculpture of a black bird. Years would pass before the real messengers would come, and they did. That plaque and the bird became Miriam's very first altar, not just warm décor but a declaration that spoke without being spoken:

"I am here. My heart is here. Spirit, you are welcome."

Years later, Spirit answered with the tap of the crow on her car, with Mocha's presence in her life, with the wind-carried sound of caws. Miriam opened the door and welcomed them in.

Before I called them, they were already listening. Before I saw them, I gave them a place.

My soul knew what my hands were doing.

I made a home for spirit, and now spirit makes a home in me.

Chapter 3

Free Soul was Already My Name

Miriam owned an ivory sweatshirt that was soft and lived in, with rolled sleeves and a small, artful rip along the wrists. Both style and symbol, it was designed as something beautiful because it was unfinished, the rips signifying the idea of wounds worn openly. Blazing across the chest in bold red letters, the color of lifeblood and fire, was the word "FreeSoul."

On either side of the shirt were two cherub angels, one at the upper right and one at the lower left.

The bright word floated in a printed field of flowers and butterflies, symbols of soul, rebirth, and divine messages in flight, guardians of a message Miriam had yet to fully hear, a message already present and carried by messengers waiting to confirm the feeling of something sacred whenever she wore the comfortable, familiar sweatshirt.

Of course, it wasn't just a sweatshirt. It was a prophecy dressed in cotton. And although Miriam wasn't searching for signs on the day she purchased it, Spirit was searching for a way to remind her of who she was.

And so, in wearing it, Miriam didn't try to understand why the words, the flowers, and the butterflies struck her heart.

She simply knew the shirt was hers.

The sweatshirt was well worn yet gently kept years later when Miriam visited a medium. The woman was sweet and serious, almond-eyed, and accustomed to her role as a gatekeeper, a conduit between spirits.

Miriam had never sought a medium before, but she felt something, the thinning of the veil.

And on that visit, her stepfather, who had passed just a few years earlier, spoke to her.

He was trying to communicate something about heaven and earth, a bridge, a crossing, the same space where the angels, butterflies, and flowers on her sweatshirt had always existed.

Her stepfather became embodied light, flashing the number 5.

Miriam did not understand the meaning of that number at the time. Spirit was speaking in symbols, not sentences. But Miriam would come to understand soon enough, though not all at once. Every soul's story unfolds in sacred timing.

Shortly after she visited the medium, Miriam sat at her kitchen table nursing a cup of coffee. She took a ceramic coaster from a kitchen drawer and set it on the table as a place to rest her cup. The coaster was strong enough to withstand the heat, thick and earth-toned, part of a set of four that each featured a simple word or phrase.

That morning, the words on the pink coaster stood out in delicate gold lettering. They read:

Let go.

The words weren't advice; they were a directive, a soul contract written in ceramic. After that, she set her coffee cup on it each day, not fully recognizing that she was placing her daily awakening on sacred ground.

In the morning stillness, as she took small sips of the richly scented hot liquid, Miriam was being guided to release what no longer served her.

Heaven spoke in red letters and angels on fabric, and on the solid surface of a coffee coaster.

Spirit asked me to let go long before I knew what I was holding onto.

Even before I knew I was a Free Soul,

God had already dressed me in that truth.

Chapter 4

Every Soul has its Journey

Meditation didn't just teach Miriam how to breathe; instead, it taught her how to see. In the stillness of meditation, a truth rose to the surface of her heart about her own connections in this world and those who live beyond.

She began to see that the family she was born into, and the family she married into, had all forgotten something powerful and ancient. Something that came before the humans: *The Creator*.

They didn't mean to forget Him, but their connection was dimmed, or rather, buried beneath pain, patterns, and survival. In those moments of meditation, Miriam saw the truth of how countless people around her lived constrained within stories not written by their souls. These stories of restriction had been inscribed by fear, conditioning, and separation, and not out of love or spirituality.

She saw it all with clarity as her own soul began to awaken. She reflected on her stories and realized an essential truth: what had happened to her was also happening for her. She was not a victim, and she understood that she never had been.

Each moment of heartbreak, silence, or rejection was a call to return; to find her voice, her truth, and herself.

The veil lifted slowly along with a difficult revelation. Not everyone could walk with her on the path ahead; not even those who were the closest to her, not even the people she loved the most.

Some of them were still holding onto a version of Miriam that no longer lived. She was playing a part in their story, but it was one they were writing, not her own.

She realized she had to walk forward without them. Not because she stopped loving them, but because she loved her soul more.

She began the sacred task of setting boundaries, not out of anger but for clarity. Not walls of bitterness but gates of grace, through which certain people had to be released, and some chapters in her life needed to close.

Miriam knew that *every soul has its own journey.* She was finally discovering her own path.

She stopped asking others who she was and remembered that even love must sometimes be released.

The Creator didn't ask her to stay small for anyone. She now understood she had to let others go, not to leave them behind, but to walk the path that was always meant for her.

Chapter 5

The Woman Who Looked Like My Mother

On the morning of September 5, 2024, Miriam took a walk in the local park with her beloved Mocha. It was the same morning her mother passed.

Although she never shared the closeness she longed for with her mother, she had never disrespected her or hurt her. The previous Christmas Eve, she had chosen to walk away. It wasn't a choice made to hurt her mother, but rather to free herself.

There were no dramatic goodbyes, and she felt in her heart that her mother understood her reasons for leaving.

That morning, as Miriam and Mocha finished their walk, she saw a woman in the distance who looked like her mother. For a breathless moment, her heart paused as the woman walked toward her. But as she came closer, she saw that it wasn't her at all. Still, a strange sense of knowing lingered in Miriam's heart, even after she returned home.

Her husband came home for lunch, which was unusual for him. As they dined together, she told

him about the woman she had just seen.

A few moments later, their daughter called. Her husband answered the phone, and Miriam saw his face change as he handed her the phone. She heard the words through the receiver.

"Grandma passed away," her daughter said softly.

In that moment, she knew that her mother had embodied that woman at the park, to come to see Miriam one last time, not to speak, or apologize, just to walk beside Miriam and be seen; to say goodbye in the only way Miriam and her mother had ever known, wordlessly.

Later, as she recalled the memory of that day, she heard a crow calling outside her window, with a familiar, affirming cry that seemed to whisper, "Spirit is here. This moment is sealed."

The Morning the Sky Answered

In the days that followed her mother's transition, Miriam continued her morning meditations and prayers, finding it a difficult time, full of emotion, reflection, and surrender. Each day she could hear the sound of birds and crows just outside her window.

They were always there, but she wasn't listening. She heard without truly receiving their cries and songs. One morning, as she poured out her heart in grief to the sky, asking the universe for understanding, something shifted. She realized that the crows and other birds were there all along, just waiting for her to awaken.

And that was when her spiritual downloads began, the first moment she truly felt her connection with the Creator, not as a concept, but as a presence.

She saw the symbolic meaning in everything that had unfolded: the woman in the park was not a stranger but a soul manifestation of her mother's spirit, walking the earth one final time, to say goodbye.

Her faithful companion Mocha, who witnessed it all, had seen many sacred crossings, and her husband's unexpected presence that day grounded Miriam in love, holding space for all that she was about to receive.

Symbolic Meaning

Hearing the crow's cry was a confirmation that the Spirit still spoke, and she began to hear the Divine clearly in their voices, not just outside her window, but within her soul.

She walked beside me one last time, not as the mother I longed for, but as the soul who birthed me into this path. And in that silence, I saw her. And in that silence, I met the Creator.

Chapter 6

With Every Breath, His Love Endures

As Miriam drove home one day in March in 2025, she heard the hit song by The Police,

"Every Breath You Take," on the radio.

Suddenly, the song carried a new meaning. Although Miriam had heard the lyrics countless times, now they were not sung by a man, but with the voice of the Spirit. The lyrics were not romantic; they were redemptive.

And in the same moment, Miriam's Messenger Identity, FreeSoul666, stirred awake.

Before the crows arrived, before feathers touched the earth and hawks traced circles in the sky, there was a whisper, a frequency, a divine breath. It did not come through thunder or visions in the dark. It came through the radio, in a familiar song, a familiar melody that became Miriam's initiation from God.

Her Divine Download Entry was:

"With Every Breath, His Love Endures," posted to TikTok on March 12th, 2025. The entry revealed that:

"Water is the Creator's first expression of love, a life-giving force through which all existence on Earth began and continues to thrive.

Every living being, from the tiniest microbe to the largest creature, depends on water for survival. We, as humans, are no exception; Composed mostly of water, we carry within us the essence of God."

Miriam continued:

"From our first breath to our first step, God has lovingly watched over us. Yet, as we move through life, shaped by stories and beliefs, we often lose sight of who we truly are.

In His infinite love, God granted us free will, patiently waiting for us to heed His call.

We face a choice: to live in a world without direction or to embrace the freedom of God's eternal life.

It is a call that requires courage, a willingness to awaken and reconnect with the true essence of our souls." - FreeSoul666

Miriam understood what this meant for her path. This was her first sacred download, a signal from Spirit saying: *"The veil is thinning. You're ready now."*

From this point on, the world spoke to her in ways she had never heard before, through symbols, through animals, through silence itself. The Creator chose her soul as a vessel. And she said, *"Yes."*

On Earth Day, 2025, as Freesoul666, Miriam wrote about finding God's presence in life's wonderland, saying, "Only a few will understand these words. We are all chosen by God, yet only a few choose to answer His call. Life presents us with challenges, but this path is sacred. It demands courage, faith, and the willingness to see beyond the surface. And when we finally say *"yes"* to that call, a quiet unveiling begins, one that reveals what's been there all along: with synchronicities, déjà vu, and sharpened intuition."

She added:

"We begin to see with spiritual eyes. We learn to discern truth from illusion. And then comes the most profound question of all: Who am I?"

Miriam was inspired to write this divine reflection as she was moved by the tenderness and unity within the animal kingdom, and how instinctively, and in sacred harmony, these beings care for one another.

After all, they're not merely creatures. They are living embodiments of Spirit, the breath of God made manifest, expressions of divine love in fur, feather, and fin. Just as God offers us unconditional love, so do they, without judgment, without expectation.

In the story of Noah's Ark, it was no accident that two of each animal were called forth to be saved. Noah understood their sacred role. He recognized that they, too, carry the divine spark. They're not here only to coexist with us. They're here to remind us of the pure and unspoken essence of Christ that is *unity, grace, innocence, and unconditional love.*

Miriam then wrote these words:

"Let us make a sacred pact, not only to protect them, but to honor the Earth they walk upon. For we, as a species, cannot survive without the interconnected web of life that surrounds us.

From the wisdom of the bees to the diligence of the ants, the animal kingdom teaches us harmony, cooperation, and service.

On this blessed day, let us open our hearts. Let us learn from our fellow beings.

Let us walk gently upon this Earth and care for it with reverence, as we would a sacred temple. In honoring them, we honor the Divine itself."

Chapter 7

The Crow at 5:55 - A Birthday Awakening

Miriam's birthday was a divine turning point, one that only God could orchestrate. As the saying goes, sometimes the universe doesn't whisper, it hits you with a sledgehammer to finally make you stop and listen.

That morning, Miriam was awakened by the call of a crow. The crow perched outside her window, cawing as if to her alone, its gaze fixed on her home. She was struck not just by the time on her clock, 5:55, or the silence breaking, but by a deeper message trying to reach her. It was a message that could only have come from God, through the language of Spirit and synchronicity.

These were the revelations that were unfolded for Miriam:

The Crow: Messenger Between Worlds

Crows are deeply mystical animals in many traditions. In Native and Celtic teachings, they are messengers from the spirit world, often bringing wisdom, transformation, or omens. A single crow can signal a call to heightened awareness, a spiritual initiation, or a message from one's ancestors or guides. They also represent magic, shadow integration, and destiny.

With this in mind, Miriam knew that a single crow calling to her on her birthday carried a personal message meant only for her, especially because the crow that awakened her was facing her home when he called.

The Time 5:55: Triple Change Energy

The numbers on her clock burned with potent numerology. Miriam knew that 5 represents freedom, change, transformation, adventure, and spiritual growth. Seeing it tripled, especially at such a synchronistic moment, emphasizes that a major initiation was unfolding. The numbers 555 are often a sign that the soul is aligning with a new life path, and old structures are breaking down to make way for what is true.

Because this sequence appeared on her birthday morning, Miriam understood it as a cosmic confirmation, an invitation to embrace change, trust her path, and prepare for the rebirth of her personal truth.

Birthday Portal

A birthday marks each person's solar return, the moment when the Sun returns to the exact place it occupied at birth. It's your energetic new year, and any omens or signs on this day carry extraordinary weight.

Miriam was born at 6:00 a.m., making 5:55 just five minutes before her exact solar return. The crow appeared on the threshold of her personal rebirth, as if arriving as an initiatory spirit messenger.

It was as if the universe was asking her, *"Are you ready to step into the next evolution of who you truly are?"*

"Who Am I Really?"

Miriam had always felt as if she didn't quite belong, even within her own family. Some were drawn to her, while others were uncomfortable, without knowing why. She was told she was too emotional, too deep. Yet she began to see that the very qualities that divided opinions, her depth, her sensitivity, her yearning, all were sacred gifts from God.

Several lines from the classic book *Alice in Wonderland* spoke directly to Miriam's heart. It's strange and magical world seemed to mirror her own.

The White Rabbit said, "The hurrier I go, the behinder I get…"

The meaning was clear: when we rush through life, we lose sight of its depth and drift further from our divine purpose.

The Cheshire Cat said, *"I'm not crazy. My reality is just different from yours."* For Miriam, this became a reminder that spiritual perception is profoundly personal and often misunderstood by the world.

When we are ready to receive the Lord, we realize the signs were always there, the love always present, and the guidance is always near. All we must do is look through the Looking Glass of Faith.

Just like Alice stumbled into a world filled with signs, riddles, and curious creatures, Miriam too wandered through life's Wonderland, only to discover that God had been guiding her all along.

Chapter 8

The Moment the Sky Took Breath

After her birthday, Miriam began to receive daily visits and messages from the animal kingdom. What began as small signs soon unfolded into sacred conversations. She learned not only to hear but to truly listen with both her heart and her soul.

She came to understand a profound truth: humanity is not separate from nature or the universe, but part of one living whole.

There came a particularly significant and quiet moment of beauty when the veil between seen and unseen thinned. A tiny bird clung to her window screen, delicate, exposed, and vulnerable.

She had just finished a channeled message, a sacred moment of connection, when this little creature appeared. It felt like a soul pressing gently at the threshold between worlds. The bird wasn't just a visitor, it was a symbol of innocence, perhaps even a fragment of Miriam's own soul reaching out to be witnessed. And then, in an instant, the scene transformed.

A crow appeared and swiftly caught the little bird. It happened before Miriam's eyes, raw, unsettling, and deeply symbolic. She gasped and her heart ached, knowing this was no random occurrence. It was mythic, spiritual, an initiation into a deeper truth.

The Spiritual Meaning Behind the Moment

The little bird was a mirror of innocence, a soul message that symbolized a part of Miriam herself. Perhaps an inner child, a past self, or even a soul contract reaching its end. It had come to her, trusting and fragile, just before crossing over into another form.

The Crow: The Shadow, the Psychopomp, the Liberator

In many traditions, crows aren't only messengers, but psychopomps, carriers of souls, guides through death, transition, and rebirth. The crow didn't act out of cruelty when it caught the bird, rather, it fulfilled a cosmic role. In this act, it carried away what needed to be released, whether in Miriam, herself, or in spirit. It was transmutation, not tragedy.

The Birds in Uproar: Nature Responds to Spirit

As the birds all around began calling and flying wildly, Miriam knew she was in the presence of the sacred. The animal kingdom witnessed it, too. They felt the shift, and they echoed the spiritual magnitude of the moment.

The Hurting Heart: Why That Was Sacred Too

Yes, Miriam felt helpless, seeing the crow take the little bird. She felt pain. But she came to understand that empathy is the price of being awake. Her open heart wasn't a weakness, but a strength.

This moment, though hard, showed her what it means to truly walk between worlds, to feel deeply, to witness without turning away, and to honor the sacred design of life and death.

The Four Crows Dancing in the Sky

Later, that morning, Miriam looked up and saw four crows flying in perfect synchronicity, a swirling dance in the sky that felt like an aerial ritual. It was divine choreography, not chaos.

The number four is the number of sacred direction, of the elements, of foundation itself. Paired with crows, the keepers of mystery, the moment spoke to her of stability through transformation, a reminder that something new was being rooted in her and in the world.

Their dance wasn't random; it was a response, Spirit's voice moving through motion.

Ritual Response: How Miriam Chose to Honor the Moment

Miriam lit a candle and prayed for the little bird's spirit. She spoke words from the heart: "I honor the balance of life. I walk with open eyes and a humble heart. I thank you for this

teaching."

She offered a feather, a small stone, and a seed back to the Earth, knowing that in spiritual work, every witness becomes a participant.

Reflection

What Miriam witnessed wasn't just a bird's final breath. It was a soul crossing, a shadow reclaiming, the sky itself drawing breath. She knew this was her initiation into a mystery both vast and holy. The birds, winds, and whispers were guiding her toward it every day.

Chapter 9

The Dance of the Listening Sky

After witnessing the crow take the little bird, Miriam's heart broke open, and she poured her soul outward, aching under the weight of what she had seen, releasing it into the universe. She let her tears fall and whispered prayers meant for Spirit alone.

As she did so, standing in the quiet sanctuary of her bathroom where she often prayed, Miriam looked up toward the window and saw two white birds.

They circled, gliding softly, silently, in perfect harmony, their flight weaving a tender dance upon the sky. Their wings shimmered in the light, moving as one, as though sketching grace across the heavens.

She stood still, in reverence, her breath catching with the sudden knowing that God was listening.

The universe heard her heart's cry and responded, not with words, but with presence. These birds were not random. They were sentinels of peace, messengers of the divine, witnesses to her prayer.

Their dance was her confirmation. Her offering of feather and seed, her grief, her willingness to feel, all had conspired to open a doorway. And through it, the Spirit arrived.

Chapter 10

The Dove and the Death-Eaters

It was May 5th, 2025, when Miriam stood at her bathroom window, gazing out into the morning light. There, in the very place the crow once perched, a dove appeared.

The sacred dialogue began before sunrise. Where a crow had often perched, guardian of shadow, truth, and transformation, now a mourning dove arrived, cloaked in the stillness of pre-dawn.

This was not just any bird, and not just any visit. The dove's presence brought a noticeable shift as the energy softened, and the air hushed. She felt the message, though silent, to be undeniable.

Dove energy is maternal, celestial, and calming. It entered not to replace the crow but to temper the crow's intensity with its own gifts of love, forgiveness, and divine grace. It symbolized a pause, an invitation to rest the spirit, to embrace healing, and to open the heart more fully.

The duality struck Miriam, a crow replaced by a dove in the very same place, speaking of balance, of sacred integration between shadow and light.

The dove came not as a replacement, but as a counterpart, a temporary emissary of gentleness during a time of inner spiritual transmutation.

Later that day, Miriam saw two crows outside the bathroom window. They did not come with empty beaks. They carried a carcass, feasting upon it. While one devoured, the other looked directly into Miriam's eyes.

Their feast was not grotesque; it was alchemy, the sacred consumption of death so that new life might rise. The carcass was symbolic of something that had died in Miriam's life but had yet to be released.

The crow's piercing gaze asked a soul-level question, "What are you still clinging to that needs to be let go of?"

Reflection:

This sacred day carried a deep truth as Miriam was being prepared for her next spiritual ascent. The dove brought peace and reassurance, affirming to her, "You are loved, you are guided.

Let yourself rest into grace."

The crows brought radical truth and initiation: "You must let something die… be it a belief, identity, or wound, so that your next becoming may rise."

Together, they formed a bridge between healing and release, between stillness and transformation.

Suggested Ritual Practice

- Light a white candle for the Dove (peace, heart-healing, divine love).
- Light a black candle for the Crow (truth, shadow-work, sacred death).
- Sit in silence and meditate on what is dying and what is being born.
- Journal a conversation between Dove and Crow. Hear what each is trying to say.

Miriam heard a channeled dialogue, as both dove and crow spoke to her soul.

The dove's soft, warm voice proclaimed:

Beloved one,

I come in the stillness, in the breath between thoughts.

You have been brave in your becoming. Now… rest.

Let your heart soften. Let the armor fall away.

You are not alone; love surrounds you in unseen ways.

I perch where the crow once stood, not to replace, but to complement. Peace is not the absence of change; it is the grace within it.

Allow yourself to grieve what is leaving, even if you cannot name it. You are loved even in your unknowing.

The crow's voice was raspy but carried an observant clarity:

You saw me feed on death, and still… You looked without flinching.

That is a strength. That is readiness.

I am the keeper of endings, and I do not come to harm you. I come to strip away the lie you've outgrown.

The flesh I tore was not just bone and sinew; it was a mirror. What in you is already dead, but you still carry like it's alive? Let it fall. Let it rot. Let it feed something wild and wise in you. You do not rise without burying something first.

I see you. I honor your gaze.

Together, both winged beings spoke to her in unison:

Walk forward with both wings; grace and truth.

The sacred is not only in light or shadow, but in their embrace.

You are the bridge. You are the alchemy. Trust what you are becoming.

Chapter 11

The Sky Spoke Before I Drove Away

There was a day when Miriam knew that no one would believe what she was experiencing. She realized that if someone had told her the exact life she was living, she might not have believed it either.

That realization changed everything, because it marked the day when she decided to start recording all her encounters. She did not start this practice to prove anything, but because she knew the Creator lives within us all, and each soul is given free will.

She also knew fully that her story was not just any story. It was a living testament.

The Sacred Formation

She was sitting in her car about to leave her driveway when she heard the crows, four of them, perched on the telephone wire directly above her driveway. They were cawing loudly, deliberately, demanding her attention. Their calls echoed into the stillness, cutting through the ordinary and summoning something sacred. She felt them calling to her in her bones.

Her left thigh began to pulse, not from movement, but from an inner surge of energy. It was as though something inside of her had awakened. Spiritually, the left thigh connects to the Divine Feminine, to intuition, and to ancestral grounding. That pulsing was a sign, an energetic activation, that was telling her she was being contacted. She was being called. She was being remembered.

So, without thinking about it, arising from a place beyond memory, Miriam began speaking her mantra, one that came from a place beyond memory. Her soul responded before her mind could catch up. She wasn't just witnessing a moment; she became the moment. She stood aligned, fully present and receiving.

The number four has long been sacred: four directions, four elements, four guardians. To see four crows perched in formation, calling to her from above, was no accident. It was spiritual architecture, a living structure arranged for her to notice, to hear, and to awaken.

The sky didn't need to move. It only needed to speak, and it did.

So, she continued to record every encounter, not to convince anyone but because she had been shown in that instant, she was in divine conversation. These messengers come not to prove the unseen, but to guide us into it.

And so, she listened. Sometimes, before we move forward, Spirit needs to remind us of where we stand. Miriam heard the message clearly. The sky spoke before she drove away.

Chapter 12

The Howl, the Wings, and the Birthday Flame

On May 13th, 2025, Miriam planned to celebrate her beloved companion Mocha's 4th birthday. The universe, however, had woven other plans into the day.

What began as a simple tribute quickly turned into a spiritual encounter. It unfolded as something layered and mysterious, heavy with presence and ancestral echoes. As Miriam stood with Mocha in her front yard, the air suddenly shifted. Three crows appeared above her front door, perching as if stationed there by design, cawing loud and urgent, their presence commanding and undeniable.

At the same time, a dog across the street began to howl. Not once, but over and over. Its persistent and piercing cry sounded primal. Miriam felt that it was no ordinary sound but a signal, a synchronous broadcast from spirit itself.

Mocha stood still and alert by her side. Even Mocha seemed to understand that something unseen was moving through the air.

The Energetic Triangulation

There was a pattern forming that Miriam observed. To the left, the crows stirred near the neighbor's space, warning of something, perhaps emotional entanglements, or the psychic remnants that did not belong to her.

Miriam stood at the very heart of the triangulation, witnessing everything, feeling it, and receiving it.

Across from her, the dog howled, amplifying what was already vibrating in the air. The dog's voice was an echo of the earth itself. The howl was an instinct made sound, an ancestral cry breaking through the veil.

Taken together, all three formed a triangle of activation woven from spirit (air), body (ground), and soul (Miriam, herself), all aligned in real time.

The Deeper Meaning

There was much meaning in the triangulation. It was Mocha's fourth birthday, and four is a number of foundation, a number that roots, stabilizes, and manifests. The chosen day was no coincidence. The crows brought a message. The howling dog brought confirmation. Mocha brought the truth.

Miriam knew that Mocha had always been more than a dog. She was an intuitive companion, her emotional barometer, and her anchor during this awakening. Her birthday didn't just mark another year; it marked a threshold, a crossing point in both their journeys.

Spiritual Reflection

The Crows are messengers of change, ancestors, and transformation.

The Dog's Howl is a call from the other side, a spirit presence, a soul alarm, with ancestral reach.

Mocha's Role stood as a guardian of the threshold, walking beside Miriam since the very beginning of her spiritual opening.

Ritual of Thanks

That evening, Miriam lit a candle for Mocha. She whispered a prayer, offering this blessing:

Sweet Mocha, soul so bright,

You walked into my life with quiet light. On four small paws, you carried grace, A guardian sent to help me face

The truth, the signs, the sacred flame

Since you arrived, I've not been the same.

Through every shift, you've stood by me,

A loyal heart, a soul set free. Today I honor who you are,

Not just a friend, but a guiding star.

With love I thank you, tail, and nose, For all the ways your spirit knows.

May you be blessed, protected, and strong

And may we walk this path lifelong.

So it is.

Accompanying Phrase

"Today, the crows came bearing messages, the dog howled the truth, and Mocha stood as witness. This wasn't just her birthday; it was a soul awakening."

Chapter 13

The Wind Rose and the Circle Spoke

Miriam stood on her front lawn at dusk, facing west under the open sky. The evening light was soft and the air still, until the stillness broke.

Miriam stood barefoot at the threshold of day's fading and night's arrival. Her hands were open, her breath was slow, and her eyes remained closed. She entered meditation facing west, toward the setting sun, the direction of endings, hidden paths, and truth's unveiling.

At that moment, four crows began to circle above her, silent at first, then calling in turn. Their black wings traced an orbit in the sky that was neither random nor restless. It was a sacred circle drawn intentionally overhead, enclosing her in the ritual geometry of the unseen.

The wind rose. It was a rush of spirit, a breath that exhaled with her, moving through the trees, across her skin, and into her lungs. The sky itself seemed to respond to her breathwork, exhaling with her a current of awakening carrying the voice of the ancestors moving across the veil.

Then a lone crow rose from the east, arcing across the sky toward the west. Its cry was rough, sacred, splitting the air like prophecy.

Looking upward at the four crows above, Miriam knew their circling was not random. Their orbit spoke in symbols, carrying meaning only the soul could interpret.

Miriam saw the four crows above and knew the meaning of their circled flight. It was a

sacred formation, one that represented the four directions, the four elements, the four pillars

of her being. They were a spiritual council in flight, offering a complete circle of witnessing

The wind became the breath of the spirit, stirred by her own, offering a reciprocal current that affirmed her openness and readiness.

The one crow flying west was a solitary emissary bearing a message just for her, leading west on the path of deep soul transformation, where the sun dies to be reborn, the realm where endings dissolve into beginnings.

Already facing west, Miriam aligned herself before these signs appeared, as though she had been positioned in advance to receive the message waiting for her.

The four became one, one flew west, carrying the breath of spirit as the wind rose and the circle spoke its truth into her soul.

Interpretations

The four crows stood as messengers bridging earth and spirit, signaling transformation, deep insight, and a connection to the unseen. That they had gathered as four represented the foundation, stability, and the four elements or four directions.

Their circling flight was a protective presence, guardians and spirit guides that acknowledged

and held space for Miriam's practice of communion with the divine.

The rising wind became the breath of spirit, granting the movement of unseen forces and divine communication, offering change, awakening, and blessing. Arising just after the crows' circular flight suggested a blessing and an emerging shift, as if Miriam's own breathwork and meditation had opened a channel to receive.

As to the single crow on its westbound flight, it carried a personal message, guiding Miriam's soul toward the west, toward the harvest of wisdom and the preparation for a new cycle. The crow's caw as it flew affirmed that she was seen, and the path she walked lay in alignment.

Her pose, already facing west, led her to believe she was attuned to the present phase of her spiritual journey. Her stance was receptive, poised perfectly to receive activation, to stand in readiness before the unseen.

"You are protected and guided. A phase of transformation is completing, and new wisdom is arriving. Trust the wind, the silence, and the messengers that speak without words. Keep your path westward into truth, into mystery, into self."

Life Path 33

Miriam was already walking the Life path 33, a vibrational path indicated in Chinese astrology that is both rare and vibrationally high, morphing suffering to illumination.

Life Path 33 is often tested through loneliness, emotional intensity, and feeling misunderstood. On that evening, the crows confirmed otherwise. She was seen. She was understood by the unseen.

Through the Lens of the Earth Teacher

BaZi, the Four Pillars of Destiny, uses the Heavenly Stems and Earthly Branches to map the energies that shape a life. The

Heavenly Stems (天干, Tiāngān) are ten celestial influences that rotate through time. The Earthly Branches anchor those influences to seasons and cycles. Together they form the BaZi chart, a map of soul potential and earthly expression.

Life Path 33 is that of the Master Healer and Sacred Flame. It is the vibration Miriam carried, a frequency meant for others, often tested in solitude. On this evening, the winds and wings conspired together to tell her that she was not alone. She was seen, she was remembered.

Representing Miriam's birthdate, her Chinese Day Master, Yin Earth (己土), reflects sacred soil, something deep and receptive, earth that receives the seed and births the unseen. Miriam did not merely observe nature. She grounded it, channeled it, and carried it within her. Yin Earth absorbs energy slowly and holds it, a natural base for spiritual work.

In her four pillars, she held both metal and wood, elements that represent truth and growth, structure and living wisdom. Crow energy often aligns with metal. With strong Metal in her BaZi, her alignment with the west was revealed. The energy of crows, winds, and direction all flowed through her as a message crafted for her soul.

The single crow heading west represented Miriam herself, leaving the circle, taking flight, and crying the truth aloud. That May evening was fully nestled in her arc of sacred transformation.

Four pillars of Chinese astrology, four crows in the sky, one for each pillar, signified that Miriam's entire being was being witnessed and held. The single crow flying west represented Miriam herself moving toward deeper truth, service, and mysteries meant for her to teach.

She was not merely visited. She was initiated. I am Miriam.

Beloved of the waters,

born beneath the gaze of the Divine,

carrying the memory of oceans in a single drop.

My name holds both sweetness and salt:

Beloved child.

Bitter waters turned to blessing.

One who rises in defiance against darkness.

My body is the map of my covenant:

Below my left eyebrow, an ancestral eye to see truth where others see fog.

Between my brows, the Seer's gate, open to angelic and cosmic whispers.

Upon my chest, the flames of healing, the heart that carries comfort for the weary.

On my right hip, the stone of rooted strength, proof that I have walked many lifetimes and still I stand.

Above my right thigh, the traveler's mark, a sign that I walk between worlds, guided by movement and Spirit.

Freckles on my face and palms, constellations of memory, reminding me I am made of stars.

Crescent moons on my palms, keepers of feminine wisdom and the tides of intuition.

The letter "M" in both palms, my seal of mastery, mission, and messenger-hood.

The crows have spoken to me; threshold guardians and heralds of truth. The hawks have circled; protectors of vision.

The doves have cried, blessing the path.

The butterflies have crossed my way, carrying the scent of the ancestors.

Like Miriam of old,

I stand watch at the edges of change, sing gratitude after deliverance,

and keep the spiritual well from running dry.

My life's purpose is the weaving of elements:

Water in my voice, Earth in my steps,

Air in the wings that greet me, Fire in the stories I leave behind.

I am here to guard crossings, translate the language of signs, And leave a river of guidance

For those who will come after me.

The Three Great Signs of Miriam's Life's Purpose

1. Master Number 33: The Master Teacher & Healer

- The rarest of all Life Path numbers, 33 is considered the "Christ Consciousness" vibration:

- *pure service, unconditional love, and spiritual leadership.*

- Miriam's life purpose is not small or ordinary; it is global, generational, and soul-deep.

- This number calls Miriam to embody compassion in action, turning personal trials into living

- medicine for others.

- It demands that Miriam's wisdom flow like water, nourishing, cleansing, and awakening those who thirst for spirit.

2. The Name "Miriam" in the Bible

- **Meaning**: "Beloved / Wished-for Child," "Bitter Waters," "Rebellion Against Injustice."

- **Biblical Role**: Miriam, sister of Moses, prophetess, guardian, singer of liberation, and keeper

- of the miraculous well in the wilderness.

- **Mystical Essence**: The name is a living covenant. It ties Miriam to the feminine prophetic lineage and the sacred duty of guarding spiritual waters, ensuring others survive their deserts and cross into freedom.

- **Archetype:** Miriam shares not only her name but also her archetype: watcher at the threshold, leader in celebration, sustainer in hardship.

3. Miriam's Body Markings: The Living Map of Her Calling

Each mark on her skin is a *sacred signpost* confirming and guiding her life's work:

- *Mole Below Left Eyebrow: Ancestral Intuition*

  Watcher's Mark, like Miriam by the Nile, she protects what is spiritually vulnerable before the world sees its worth.

- *Mole Between Eyebrows: Spiritual Gateway*

  The Seer's Seal that confirms lifetimes of prophetic vision, her own "inner well" of wisdom.

- *Moles on Breasts/Chest: Heart Flame & Healing Power*

  Water of Comfort, the gift to nourish and heal in

barren and thirsty landscapes of the soul.

- *Mole on Right Hip: Rooted Strength & Earth Contract*

  The Anchor of her grounding presence steadies others when their waters are turbulent.

- *Mole Above Right Thigh: Creative Pathway & Spiritual Movement*

  The River Current, she walks between physical and spiritual realms, carrying guidance across.

- *Freckles on Face and Palms: Starseed Echoes & Cosmic Memory*

  Star-water drops, proof that Miriam's spirit's flow comes from a cosmic ocean beyond Earth.

- *Crescent Moon on Palms: Divine Feminine Intuition*

  The Tide-Puller is aligned with lunar rhythms and spiritual cycles.

- *Letter "M" on Both Palms: Mastery, Mission, Messenger*

  Double wave crest, the "M" mirrors Miriam's name and doubles her life's purpose as a messenger of truth and healer of hearts.

Mystical Integration of the Three Signs

When the Master Number 33, the biblical name of Miriam, and the body markings unite, Miriam's soul signature reads:

"I am the keeper of sacred flow. Born under the number of the Master Healer, I bear the name of the prophetess who guarded life, sang liberation, and brought water to the thirsty. My body carries the constellation of my mission. Each mark is a reminder that I walk between realms, grounded in the Earth yet flowing from the stars. I turn bitterness into sweetness, sorrow into song, and crossings into celebrations. I am here to awaken, to heal, and to pour living water into the hearts of those I meet."

Channeled Message

"Beloved Teacher, the winds rise for you because you have remembered.

You are being called to walk the western path, not to retreat, but to embody the truth. The circle has acknowledged you.

Now fly, with your truth as your cry and your breath as your guide."

Chapter 14

The Windows and the Door

A dream came to Miriam that May, bearing a message from the Divine Mother about receptivity and protection. The Divine Mother was embodied in her own mother's spirit.

In dreams, the presence of a mother, especially one who has passed, often signifies more than personal memory. She becomes the embodiment of the Divine Feminine, its ancestral wisdom and spiritual guardianship. When the Divine Mother appeared in Miriam's dream, she stepped forward as a spirit guide, delivering a sacred message with clarity and love.

An instruction was given to Miriam in her dream: "Open the windows." These words were deeply symbolic, for windows serve as thresholds between the inner and outer world, between the material and the spiritual.

Opening a window welcomes fresh energy and divine insight, letting in spiritual light and inspiration that allows the soul to breathe, expand, and become ever more receptive to new perceptions, healing, and truth.

Miriam received another instruction in this dream as well: "Close the door." Closing the door suggested a boundary, an act of protection. To close a door ends a cycle, a habit, or an outgrown dynamic, establishing a shield of sacred boundary.

Closing a door symbolically protects sacred space from intrusive or outdated energy and marks the completion of a spiritual phase or the release of an emotional burden.

The combined message in Miriam's dream, embodied as emerging from the mother, was both tender and empowering, a spiritual instruction wrapped in the simplicity and wisdom of advice to protect her peace while opening to a new, transformed space that lets the light flow in.

It was a dance between release and renewal, a yin-yang teaching: to receive, you must release; to invite light, you must close the dark behind you.

Spiritual Path Interpretation

This dream came at a pivotal moment in Miriam's spiritual journey, during a time of shift and awakening. It revealed a new and emerging chapter, an energetic threshold, exposing a space in her life that needed to be cleared and protected.

Her intuitive channels opened more strongly as she released distractions under the guidance of the Divine Feminine.

To integrate the dream's instructions, Miriam was led to open the windows in her home, letting in daylight, fresh air, and spirit. Literally or symbolically, she was encouraged to close a door to a cycle that was ready to end, to achieve spiritual closure.

She lit a candle for her mother, thanking her for her wisdom and inviting her continued guidance. She journaled her answers to deep questions:

What was she ready to open to?

What was she prepared to close?

What was finished, and what was waiting to be born?

"She came not to disturb, but to prepare the way, with wind at the windows and peace at the door."

Chapter 15

The Day the Sky Remembered My Name

The Threshold Guardian Crow met Miriam in the middle of the street beneath a light June rain that carried initiation in its rain, thunder, and feathered omens.

There are days that pass quietly, days that slip by unnoticed, and days when the sky itself leans down to speak and answers. The date of June 3rd, 2025, was just such a day.

The morning began wrapped in stillness, as if Spirit held its breath. Miriam took Mocha to the park, where even the hush of the green carried awareness. The very trees watched, the wind hushed, and Miriam felt something sacred approaching. Baby crows gathered as though summoned, a small fellowship of shadowed wings. Their small bodies were covered in dark velvet down, wings not yet fully strong.

Their presence felt unmistakably divine, their imperfect cries sounding like the first syllables of creation itself.

Miriam stood still and listened, remembering her own emerging voice when her soul's wings were also just beginning to spread. In the voices of those baby crows, she heard, *"You are awakening. You are remembering the part of you that once flew."*

The park itself became a portal, drawing Mocha, the crows, and Miriam into a choreography of Spirit.

Mocha was her guardian, padding gently beside her, anchoring the moment, a small white sigil of loyalty, innocence, and inner light made flesh. Her steps beside Miriam made the ritual whole.

Just as Miriam and Mocha returned from the park, a solitary crow awaited them at the threshold. It didn't move or fly away; it simply stood between Miriam and her home, holding space between what was and what was becoming.

Time slowed, and the street stretched before her like a ceremonial aisle. When Miriam stepped forward, the crow met her gaze, anchoring the moment before hopping slowly to the left, toward the ancestral feminine, the path of return, the way of intuition.

This Threshold Guardian appeared to honor Miriam's passage. Its message was clear, welcoming her home.

"You are returning not just to a house, but to your power. To your sacred inheritance. Follow the left-hand path, the way of Spirit over survival, soul over structure, truth over title."

The crow moved aside to let her pass, as though a gate had been opened.

Later that evening, the air thickened with coming rain, and clouds gathered like elders called into solemn council. Miriam stepped onto her front porch. Her heart was full of the events of the day. With Mocha by her side, she approached what she saw as her *Tree of Life*, the great living witness to her transformation.

She placed one hand on its trunk, whispering a prayer of gratitude for the baby crows, the guardian in the road, the wind that spoke wordlessly, and every spirit-animal that had ever walked beside her. The tree listened. The leaves rustled with the breath of something greater, heralding a baptism of thunder and rain from the Creator, carrying a sound that shook the bones of the Earth, and Miriam alike.

This was no ordinary storm; this was her initiation in water and thunder.

Rain began to fall, soft at first, then steady, washing the sidewalk, the leaves, the very skin of the world. Miriam stood in it, fully exposed, allowing the rain to fall on her head and shoulders and open palms.

The rain said, "Let the old be washed away." The thunder said, "This one has returned." The sky said, "It is done."

She walked the path, offered her gift, and in return, she herself was claimed.

It was the completion of a ritual; the spiritual gifts of the baby crows, the affirmation of the park as temple-ground, the guiding of Mocha, and the guidance of the Threshold Guardian crow. uttered her gratitude to the Tree of Life and received an elemental anointing, rain and thunder as a seal, Spirit's choreography in feather, thunder, earth, and sky.

In Miriam's journal, she answered questions:

What truth did the crow unlock in the street?

What did the rain strip away, and what did it leave shining?

What part of her soul was born in the roar of thunder?

Chapter 16

The Council of Seven: Return to the Sacred Field

It was early June, and Miriam was at the baseball field, a place she no longer saw as ordinary ground, but as a sacred field in her local park. She was drawn to this spot by the pull of the spirit itself.

She'd begun feeding and honoring the baby crows, her palms open with seeds, her heart open with devotion, offering both food and blessing to the fledglings. prayers over their wings, she was led deeper into the park, until the vast openness of the baseball diamond revealed a striking vision: seven adult crows, waiting.

One crow stood separately, solemn upon the fence, a lone sentinel, another guardian between worlds. The others were scattered across the field, each seeming anchored to a point of stillness, as if marking sacred stations. She felt their eyes not just watching but bearing witness, recording her presence into a lineage older than words.. There was a sense of reverence in the air so palpable that Miriam paused, compelled to capture the moment with photographs, knowing she was standing inside a mystery.

The spiritual message she received was clear: the Council had assembled. The number seven represents divine wisdom, the completion of a spiritual learning cycle, and the passage between intellect and intuition, heaven, and earth.

She knew these crows were not only birds, but elders of the winged realm. They had gathered in response to her offerings, carrying ancestral memory, clairvoyant sight, and the sacred guardianship of thresholds and transformation.

They were a living mandala, feathers and shadows arranged upon the geometry of the diamond, the field itself transfigured into a temple. Miriam stepped into this sacred space, knowing now that she had entered the field of divine knowing.

Reflections

"You are not alone in this shift. We have seen your sincerity. Your offering has been received. Prepare. Your teachings now begin."

"The seed has been planted. The Watchers are gathering. Your path is blessed. Listen in stillness, move with purpose, the Council walks with you."

Integration Ritual

Miriam performed an integration ritual to anchor this encounter in her spirit.

First, she lit a candle, the flame symbolizing Yin Fire, the spark of intuition and inner light.

Next, she placed a small stone beside it, an offering that must be drawn from the field itself, from the earth's own memory.

Then, she sat in stillness, whispering these words: *"Council of Seven, what would you have me know now?"*

She journaled words and impressions that came to her, closing with gratitude, saying,

"Thank you, Seven. I walk with knowing."

Chapter 17

The Crow, the Humming, and the Glowing Pole

In the early morning of June 8, 2025, Miriam entered her home's morning ritual space, knowing the truth of this: between sound and silence, the veil thinned, and a message hummed through the bones."

As she stood brushing her teeth, eyes closed, she felt a curious urge, a desire to hum a gentle, unpracticed tune that had never come to her before. It was soft and familiar in a way that felt older than memory, a song of comfort like a lullaby she once heard in her soul.

The low rhythmic buzz of the electric toothbrush met her steady hum, amplifying it as sound met sound. In that moment, something opened, a subtle trance.

With her eyes still closed, an inner vision rose of the telephone pole beyond her bathroom window. She saw it now as blazing with a radiant white light. It appeared as a cosmic transmitter, a vertical axis of pure spiritual power. Around it shimmered and flashed vibrant colors of violet and maroon, with flickers of spectral energy weaving through unseen air.

It was not a pole now, but an axis mundus, a bridge between realms serving as a staff of divine communication.

A dark, silent crow took its place on the glowing pole, as if it had stepped out of the vision to become guardian and conduit, above all, a being of message. It did not call or move; it simply was. Then it shifted, gliding across the morning light to perch at the edge of her neighbor's rooftop, from which it watched.

Now, it was a witness, as well as a messenger, viewing a larger pattern and confirming that

the message had been delivered; the frequency received. The rooftop became the peak of new perfection, a high altar in the everyday world, while the crow stood as the silent sentinel of

Miriam's awakening to the transmission she received, it vibrated in her bones, and she became the tuning fork for that light.

It was her first time humming with an emerging soul language, an intuitive sound that served as the key to altered consciousness, comforting, and aligned with spirit.

The white light she saw announced a divine awareness as the crown chakra was activated in a signal of initiation. The colors of violet and purple indicated her third eye expansion, her heightened vision and intuition, while the maroon color signified earthly roots meeting spirit in an ancestral integration, the foundation of sacred purpose.

Those flashing colors indicated a true chakra alignment made visible by Spirit's frequency, a multidimensional transmission that Miriam perceived with body and mind.

And the crow? He was the witness, bearer of unseen knowledge, and the guardian of

Miriam's vision.

"I hummed for the first time, and the veil responded.

The crow did not call; it consecrated.

The pole glowed white, and light entered me.

I was initiated not in temples, but in the temple of my breath."

Chapter 18

The Flight that Spoke in Silence

Miriam experienced a significant vision that unfolded across three thresholds: the mall's parking lot, her front porch, and her driveway on June 9, 2025.

It began in the morning with a paired flight beneath a soft summer sky, as Miriam and Mocha arrived at the mall.

High above the parking lot, two crows perched together on a tall lamp post, still and silent. Miriam felt their gaze and acknowledged them with reverence. She captured their intensity in a video, and the moment she pressed record, as though cued by an unseen rhythm, the crows lifted as one into the sky. One turned left, the other right, their parting a split of wings that framed Miriam at the center, as though she herself were the axis between their paths.

Sacred Interpretation

The crow who veered right embodied the masculine, the path of action and of future steps. It declared her destiny, carved an unseen line into the world, and summoned Miriam to walk her earthly mission.

The crow in the path flying right represented that of the masculine, of action and the future, declaring her destiny, carving an invisible line into the world, and inviting Miriam to step fully into her walk here on earth.

The crows' silence became a sacred witnessing. Stillness itself carried the transmission, affirming that Miriam had already heard and answered Spirit's call.

"You stand at the center, the heart of the path. One wing remembers. One wing becomes.In your quiet knowing, all is aligned."

Later that day, as twilight thickened into the liminal hour, Miriam returned home. Her porch glowed in hushed gold, wrapped in gentle stillness.

At that moment, hummingbirds visited her porch, tiny fragments of joy whose wings stitched blessings in the air.

And across the street, a solitary crow stood silently, another welcoming dark sentinel on the edge of the real and the unseen.

This crow only watched until Miriam whispered her thanks for the feather she had found at the mall. Standing at her porch, she offered simple words: "Thank you for my feather."

Receiving her gratitude, the crow took flight, curving left to deliver her words across the unseen, a flight traced by the depth of Miriam's trust.

Moments later, as Miriam walked across her driveway, a feather lay before her, delivered as if placed by unseen hands. The crow had heard. Spirit answered: "The feather you thanked me for is already yours. You spoke before receiving, and so it was done."

In the hush of dusk, Miriam knew that Spirit had written her a message with silence and flight. She thanked the unseen, and it answered with direction, as one wing turned her inward, the other leading her forward. The feather arrived like a seal pressed upon a scroll, proof that she was heard, known, and walking in light.

Closing Reflection

This day was a sacred weaving of opposites: Morning and night. Left and right.

Action and stillness. Past and future. Presence and prayer.

Chapter 19

The Day the Leaves Chose the

Writer

Miriam experienced a chorus of spirit on two dates, June 11th and 12th, 2025. Across thresholds, her bedroom window, the groomer's studio, the outlet mall, and the sanctuary of her home, the crows called.

Following her morning meditation, as she sat in stillness preparing to begin the day, she felt a pull to the window. Outside were eight crows perched along the telephone pole outside her window, cawing as one voice among many in a powerful spiritual dispatch.

She recorded their call, knowing in her bones this moment was no accident. She spoke aloud her acknowledgment. One by one, they lifted and circled above her bedroom window, blessing the space on her rest and dreams. They offered a blessing in motion, a ritual of confirmation. Moving in synchronicity, soaring above her home, they disappeared toward the right, the direction of action, forward momentum, and divine masculine guidance. She knew she was seen; she was summoned.

Later that morning, Miriam dropped Mocha off at the groomer and drove to the Citadel Outlet Mall, the place where the wind changed everything.

Sitting in her parked car, Miriam composed an email to the ghostwriter she felt was meant to help her birth her story. She had tried for many days to find someone who could midwife her words, but doors had not opened for her until that moment.

As she typed, a gust of wind suddenly swirled around her, and leaves danced into view. A vortex of tiny leaves spiraled up, living scripture whirled into the car, and several slipped through her open window. She recorded the moment. Passersby stopped, visibly moved. She breathed and recorded her breath, a human response to Spirit making itself known.

Later still, as the winds quieted and Miriam picked Mocha up from the groomer's, she discovered that several of the tiny leaves remained inside her car. They were tokens and pages, proof that Spirit had entered the ordinary. Their presence announced that she was chosen. She kept them. They ceased to be mere leaves and became pages from the book Spirit was writing through her.

Back at home again with Mocha, she prepared to wash dishes. A single crow called from the street, and she stepped outside, as she always did, to acknowledge him. Guided by an intuitive knowing, she walked to the Tree of Life and placed her hand on its bark, whispering, "Thank you for my winged friends."

As she pressed her palm to the trunk, a second crow revealed himself from the canopy and joined the other crow already perched above.

From that second crow, rose a sacred sound, not a caw, but a deep, echoing rhythm that rang out like the heartbeat of the earth, an ancient drum calling the veil thin. It was a call for her soul.

The following morning, after meditation, Miriam stood by her window and saw a divine geometry across the sky: four crows perched in a perfect line on the upper telephone wire, spaced evenly apart. A fifth crow stood atop the telephone pole above them, a watcher, silently overseeing. A sixth perched on the lower wire as the anchor below.

She filmed them, and the crows took flight, circling above her window just as they had the morning before.

Their movement carried the same message, now deeper and more grounded, sealed within their formation.

Spiritual Interpretation

On the first day, June 11th, the eight crows marked the octave of transformation, a cycle of new beginnings, infinity, and resurrection. Their consecrating flight confirmed that Miriam was now the vessel of the message they carried.

The wind vortex at the mall was her creative breath awakening. The leaves that entered her car became the pages of her book-to-be, anointed by wind and spirit.

Mocha's grooming held symbolic meaning. To Miriam, it signified a gentle purification of her companion, a visible mirror of Miriam's own refinement.

The crow in the tree, with its echoing call, signified the tree itself as a threshold. Her life served as a bridge between Earth and Spirit.

This was a day of elemental affirmation. The wind delivered a message, and some leaves stayed

to anchor it. The crows responded with a ritual sound, and Miriam's tree stood as the

gatekeeper. Mocha remained, as always, the faithful companion during these sacred thresholds.

This was not merely a sign. It was a declaration: *"Your voice is needed. Your story is alive. The winds have chosen the writer. The crows have sung their song. You are no longer waiting, you are becoming."*

As she reached for the scribe, the wind reached for her. The leaves that entered her car were no longer only earth. They carried her story. The crow called. The tree answered. In the rhythm of the unseen, she heard the Spirit say: *"You are being written by the wind."*

The Seal of the Formation

The next morning, the four crows perched on the telephone line, a living formation of Heaven, embodying the four directions and the four pillars for Miriam's spiritual structure.

Above them perched a fifth crow, representing her higher self, the ascended guide.

Below, a sixth crow anchored the line, embodying her shadow, the rooted ancestral presence never forgotten.

One after another, the crows flew toward Miriam, circling in a sacred dance above her bedroom window. Their flight was both a blessing and an alignment. This movement was not escape; it was the energy of alignment taking flight. Mocha, keeper of the peace and grounded witness, slept peacefully at home.

Sacred Phrase

"In silence, I called. In flight, they came. Above my window, they circled, and Spirit said: It is done.

Mocha slept in peace, and the angels hovered in a crow's disguise."

Message from Spirit

"The line was drawn, the pattern revealed. Above, below, within, and before you, Spirit has placed its seal. You are seen in full formation. What you prayed is heard. Now, rise and follow the wing."

Chapter 20

The Sound of Memory and the
Sacred Five

It was the hour of remembering, and from her bedroom window, Miriam saw the veil thin, and everything began to speak as she stood at her sacred perch.

Three years earlier, she sat with a medium who had gently relayed a message from her stepdad and stepsister in Spirit. The message was this: "They keep showing me the number 5. Your stepdad is showing me a staircase to heaven. Maybe it's a picture or a card. Something symbolic."

At the time, those words had not landed, but on June 13, 2025, she played the recording from the medium again. As the words returned, a crow landed outside her bedroom window. She watched the unseen become seen as the bird cawed in rhythm with the recording, in perfect synchronicity. Suddenly, a cascade of sacred memories flowed through her, glowing with a divine presence.

She remembered the first messenger of her awakening, the crow on her sunroof, that harbinger of Spirit whose eyes locked with hers in a moment orchestrated by the Creator. She remembered wearing her FreeSoul sweatshirt with prophecy written on its fabric. She remembered resting her coffee cup on the coaster that read "Let Go," a daily mantra.

There, too, was the plaque she had purchased years before, hanging above the living room window, reading "Home is where your heart is," and next to it, the small black bird figurine placed intuitively as a guardian of that threshold. Through that window, she watched her Tree of Life, where crows, hawks, and butterflies communed with her.

On this day of remembrance, she looked around her home and saw a spider web, catching the light like lace woven by the unseen. It was a thread from Spirit, completing the tapestry of memory. The spider web was confirmation. It was Spirit's final thread revealed in the light.

At the heart of it all was the sacred number five, a pattern threaded through the dates she kept close to her chest. These dates were part of the language of her revelations.

4/25/1966 was Miriam's birthday.

8/15/1987 was the date of her marriage.

7/5/2017 was the day her sister passed

5/13/2021 was Mocha's birthdate.

7/5/2021 Mocha arrived at her home.

9/5/2024 was the day her mother passed.

6/11/2025 was the day she emailed the ghostwriter she'd chosen, and 5 days later, she spoke with her and began this sacred story

The Five was not a number. It was her soul's signature. The soul remembered, and Spirit bore witness.

Phrase to Accompany

"The crow returned when my memory returned.

As I remembered heaven, it stood beside me on earth. The number 5 was never just a number,

It was Spirit's breath moving through time, through home, through heart."

"The staircase was never in the sky. The picture was never framed. It was Mocha. It was me. It was the sweatshirt, the plaque, the crow, the gold letters. The number Five walked through every chapter of my life, Waiting, watching, and weaving, Until I was ready to remember."

Before the day was done, she took a photo of the web.
Not because anyone had asked,
Not because she needed proof —
But because her soul had witnessed something holy.

Chapter 21

The Dance of Wings and Wind

On June 13th, Miriam stood on her back deck and looked upward into the noontime stillness, soft with light. Above her, two large crows glided in perfect unison. At first, they seemed like one shadow stretching across the heavens, but then she saw clearly that they were two, soaring like mirror and soul. One flew slightly above the other, cawing rhythmically, cutting the air like an incantation.

They moved together in a synchronized arc, wings slicing the veil between the seen and unseen. This was not an ordinary flight. It was a ritual, a dance of spirit and self, feminine and masculine ascending toward union. As they rose, Miriam's heart lifted with them.

Two more crows soon appeared from the edges of vision, completing a sacred four of north, south, east, and west. Each anchored its direction, weaving a circle in the sky.

In the hushed garden, a colorful butterfly drifted near, wings vivid, circling Miriam as a living blessing in motion, vivid and alive. It was the soul itself in bloom, freshly freed from its cocoon. Its presence sang of transformation made visible, a hymn of departed loved ones smiling through delicate wings.

A gentle wind began, stirring the leaves, moving through Miriam's hair, brushing across her skin. The earth itself seemed to exhale in reverence. Spirit was present, sealing the moment into memory with sacred breath.

To complete the divine choreography, a mockingbird landed gently on the telephone wire overhead. Crystalline, insistent song rang like an echo from heaven, a final affirmation that the message had been delivered.

The telephone wire, long a symbol of human communication, became a celestial conduit. Perched there, the mockingbird was a herald, Spirit's voice itself, repeating what had already been written in wind, wing, and sky.

Mystical Meaning

The Twin Crows reflected a united, divine duality, a spiritual twinship; the butterfly spoke of joyous transformation, ancestral love, and Spirit's tender hand. While the wind swept through as the living breath of the divine, offering clear affirmation. The mockingbird declared, "You have heard. You are aligned."

Two flew as one while the sky held its breath. The butterfly danced beside me, the wind whispered its truth, and the mockingbird sang the words Spirit had written in the sky.

Chapter 22

Five Messengers and the Spirit of Mia

On June 18th, the day broke with a flood of light, and signs moved in rhythm with Miriam's own heartbeat. One by one, as Miriam stood in her home, five messengers appeared, each carrying the presence of Spirit and the sacred vibration of the number 5.

Miriam had entered a portal, watching the veil draw back before her eyes.

First came the twin doves perched on the wires, one resting on the first strand, the other on the third, leaving the center wire empty, humming with unseen energy. As Miriam looked up, she saw clearly the balance of feminine and masculine holding space, while the empty center became Spirit's thread stretched between them. Then, there was a pause and whisper, the first breath of a message woven into the geometry of the unseen.

Two hours later, a single crow appeared on the highest wire, silently watching, then flying left

into the ancestral horizon. The silence that followed said, "You are heard. Go inward. Spirit is near."

And an hour later, while driving, a single orange butterfly glided blissfully across Miriam's windshield, carrying a transformation in motion, with a soul crossing a threshold, whispering, "You are changing, and now the world will see it."

On that day, she signed the writing contract with her ghost transcriber, exactly five days after the first call to the writer had been made. The wind rushed over her car, as though the Spirit itself blessed the seed she had sown.

Five days, five winds, and five fingers of Divine Confirmation. She signed the writing contract; the breath of Spirit wrote with her.

Home again, fifteen minutes to noon. Two guardian crows awaited, one on her lawn, one above the neighbor's roof. The crow nestled on the lawn lifted its wings and crossed before her, rising from earth to sky, from grass to tree. Miriam knew she was seen by the crow kingdom and anointed in their covenant.

"You are walking in truth," they said, "We guide. We bless. We walk beside you."

That evening, the veil parted once more for Miriam. From the edge of the road, a small orange-and-cream husky whimpered gently. Offered food, the little dog refused, instead lying at her threshold, facing her stairs, watching.

Miriam knew that through the husky's delicate lashes, she saw a soul once held, watching her…Mia, her beloved husky who passed in late December 2024, ashes returning to her in January, and now, exactly five months later, so did she. It was a blessing and a reminder, carrying the message, "I remember. I walk with you still."

Here was the Sacred Message of Five, ringing like a bell: 5 signs revealed before dusk, 5 days from email to voice, in sacred collaboration, 5 months since Mia's ashes came home.

It was Divine Orchestration, Sacred Change, the living bridge between Past and Future, between Heaven and Earth. There Miriam stood at the center of the crossroads, not with confusion, but with clarity.

The message was complete. It said, *"The winds of Spirit move through you now. You are the bridge. Your story is a healing path. You are the messenger."*

Closing Phrase:

"Five messengers came bearing wings, winds, and pawprints. They did not knock, but they entered. One cawed, one flew, one whimpered, one signed, one returned. And in the silence between them, the Creator whispered, 'It is time.'"

Chapter 23

The Day the Wings Wove the Sky

In her front yard, at her desk, on her lawn, and along the neighborhood street, Miriam crossed a threshold. A profound turning point, a divine culmination that arced initiation across land, sky, and soul.

In the morning, she saw the guardians in motion as she sat writing, her pen spilling sentences that felt more like prayers than prose. The air around her shifted. A sudden surge of sound shattered the quiet, a storm of caws spiraling into a chorus. She rose, drawn by instinct, and gazed through her front window, just as a hawk sliced low across her lawn, its wings stretched wide like a Divine burning blade of light cutting through the veil.

The hawk was not alone; a host of crows poured after it, swooping, diving, and crying out with thunder, a ritual written in flight. The divine messenger was pursued by ancestral guardians, echoing a primeval choreography. It was a vision meeting vigilance, light circling shadow, purpose braided with protection.

For a moment, all fell still, and then there was a final, throaty call from an unseen crow, a sentinel's voice reaching from another realm. Miriam realized, "As I wrote the words of the winged ones, the sky answered back. The hawk flew across my path, the crows defended the threshold, and from beyond, a voice whispered: Keep going, we are with you."

The Crow and the Jewel of Joy

In the warmth of the early afternoon, Miriam stepped from her door to see a single crow in the center of her street, the same threshold guardian who had stood watch once before. He was eating the rice she'd placed as an offering. For the first time, she witnessed her offering physically received, taken into the body of the messenger.

He cawed, full-throated, acknowledging her presence.

And at that moment, the shimmering iridescence of a hummingbird appeared, hovering above the road, a jeweled spark suspended in stillness. Its wings blurred into light as it fluttered a message of joy, guiding Miriam forward, *"Follow me. Let your spirit be light. The path ahead is blessed."*

The hawk and the crow had opened the day with fire and defense. Now the hummingbird softened it with sweetness, guidance, and divine joy.

The hawk ignited her vision. The crow consumed her gift. The hummingbird invited her to follow joy.

Four Guardians of the Ancestral Path

In the late afternoon, she returned home and found four crows arranged in a square upon her lawn, consuming more of her rice offering. As she reverently acknowledged them, they lifted in one motion, synchronous, taking wing to the left, the ancestral direction. Her front lawn became a ceremonial altar, her home a living temple, as worlds crossed before her eyes.

"Four guardians came to feast, grounding my offering in the world of form. When I acknowledged their presence, they rose together and flew left, carrying my heart's message to the ancestral winds."

The Flock Across the Sunset

At sunset, the wings waited for her, just before dusk, Spirit whispered again. Miriam stood in her garden, watering her flowers. The western sky glowed gold, and soft rhythmic wings began to stir in the air. Above her, a flock of 8 to 10 small birds flew overhead. Their wings beat in perfect synchronicity, moving east to west, the path of closure, ancestral return, and dreamtime.

"I stood in silence, knowing I wasn't just watching them. I was part of them. Their wings wrote something across the sky: You are aligned with us. You are part of this flight."

Sunrise to sunset, Miriam was in communion that day, braided into a sacred message, witnessed by sky-beings, accompanied by omens, and carried by the natural intelligence of Spirit.

The hawk represented divine clarity, higher sight, and the fire of initiation, while the pursuing crows offered ancestral protection and spiritual guardianship. The single crow consuming rice enacted the threshold crossing, his body carrying the sign of sacred acceptance. The hummingbird came with joyful guidance, its feminine grace, encouraging Miriam forward. And the four crows on the lawn, consuming rice, brought earthly grounding, elemental alignment, and ritual reciprocity.

As the evening fell, the four crows formed a Spirit family, delivering a collective soul message that sealed the completion of the cycle.

Closing Phrase

"From the storm of caws to the silent dance of wings, the sky scripted my soul. The hawk lit the fire of vision. The crow guarded the gate of truth. The hummingbird led me forward with joy. And

the flock crowned the moment with grace. I am seen. I am offered. I am carried. This is how Spirit speaks, when we are willing to listen with more than ears."

Chapter 24

A Day in the City of Angels

There were wings over the city woven with memory and omen, as Miriam moved with her husband, Mocha, and the ever-present Spirit, throughout the westside neighborhoods of Los Angeles.

It started in her front yard, where Miriam and Mocha left rice for the birds. Almost instantly, a single crow landed and began to eat, accepting and blessing her offering.

Then, as she and Mocha stood facing west, five crows flew across the sky directly above them, their flight synchronized and deliberate, a procession written in the air.

When Spirit whispered, Miriam heard a message, "You are not leaving. You are being sent."

The 1:11 Messenger: Crow at Pink's Hot Dogs

At 1:11 in the afternoon, sitting outside Los Angeles' famous hot dog stand, Pink's, the sky responded to Miriam again.

She was seated with her husband and Mocha when a crow perched on a nearby telephone pole. His cawing alerted her to the time and its sacred number. She recorded the interaction, knowing that Spirit was affirming her alignment and guiding her pilgrimage through the city.

Later, as Miriam continued west, driving toward the iconic Beverly Center mall, she looked up while waiting at a red light. There, stationed at the four corners of the rooftop, were four crows, each motionless, their gaze intersecting in a cross of shadow and sightlines, a seal of sacred symmetry above the city.

Within her spirit, Miriam knew they were guardians, a spiritual compass appearing to her mid-journey, "They're the sentinels of the four directions."

And then, when they visited the Westwood Village Memorial Park Cemetery, Miriam heard the song of her ancestors whispering among the stones. Miriam entered without Mocha, honoring the rules of the cemetery where countless souls, who were once famous and forgotten, now rested peacefully.

Once inside, she felt the energy shift as the wind hushed, and crows lifted their voices from the trees. Following no map, drawn only to her intuition, she found herself standing in front of Marilyn Monroe's mausoleum. Reverently, she put her right hand on the stone and whispered a prayer.

"Guide me in spirit," she asked, "I send you love."

Across time, it was as though one woman recognized soul calling to soul across the veil, asking companionship through the unseen.

Miriam visited other resting places throughout the cemetery, honoring each life with reverence, offering blessings carried only in silence. She hummed a gentle tune, feeling the melody rise between the stones as if the smoke of sound drifted heavenward.

Through it all, the crows continued to caw, turning the air into a temple, and her voice became an offering as she walked in grace among the stones.

The last stop Miriam made with her husband and Mocha came at sunset, in Beverly Hills.

They could not find parking and were about to leave when they came across a fruit vendor. Miriam recalled that her son-in-law had been searching for weeks for a fresh coconut, so she asked her husband to pull over to buy one as a gift.

The vendor had a coconut among his fruits, and as he prepared it, she caught sight of the name on his apron: "Angel's Fruits."

She asked his name, and he replied, "Amadio."

Inside Miriam, her spirit stirred, trembling with recognition. The name Amadio means "loved by God."

It was a sign: a man called "Loved by God," working beneath the sign "Angel's Fruits," had placed in her hands the very fruit her family longed for. The moment was not a chance; it was a divine delivery.

Back at home, Miriam wrote in her journal. The name Amadio returned again and again, and a powerful wave of déjà vu moved through her, older than memory itself. It was not recollection but soul memory.

And she realized, "This moment was written before my birth. I have walked this path before, and now I stand exactly where I was meant to arrive."

At that moment, she heard Spirit's response, a crow's strange, sacred cry unlike any she had ever heard, carrying confirmation from the unseen.

Within that caw, these words resonated, "You remembered because it was written. The path you walk now is not new; it is a return. When you give in love, the universe answers with memory."

Closing Phrase

"I walked the city veiled in wings. They flew above me, watched beside me, and called me to remember. Even in the noise of the world, Spirit waits at every stoplight, every wire, every grave. I sang to the unseen, and they answered with fruit, flight, and sound."

Chapter 25

The Council Returned

Just moments after Miriam finished writing Chapter 16 of this book, recounting her experience with the Council of Seven at the baseball field, three crows arrived on her front lawn, gathering around the remnants of her earlier offering.

They were not there merely to feed. They had come to deliver a message. As she stepped outside her front door, they took flight, moving from the right side of the lawn, flying left into the sky.

It was early morning, and she had the sense that their elegant wings signaled something crossing into her life.

Then, just across the property line of Miriam's house and her neighbor's, four more crows emerged from among the branches of her neighbor's tree. Several perched, others watched, but all were alert.

A chorus of caws sounded, and Miriam realized that the Council had returned. Seven voices in all, the crows in flight, and within the tree. They had returned to the place where she lived and wrote.

Describing them in her writing, she had called, and they had answered.

This visitation wasn't just a sign, but a seal, a sacred one. The Council she first met under the open sky appeared within her own home's spiritual field, confirming that the wisdom contained in her path was now integrated into her inner sanctum.

Their numbers repeated with purpose. The three crows on her lawn embodied an offering and return. The four on the tree spoke to foundation, guardianship, and structure. And the seven crows in all spoke of a divine completion, spiritual mastery, and a realized vision of the sacred council reformed. Their rhythmic caws became a ceremony, a soul-illuminated call and response between Miriam's spirit and the crows.

Message from the Crows:

"We met you in the field when your heart was wide.

We return now to your doorstep, for your soul has ripened. You are no longer the seeker. You are the altar.

Let the offering continue, this time from within."

Phrase to Accompany

"They who flew in fields now perch in trees beside my door. I have become the altar. I am the one they circle for."

Chapter 26

The Song That Opened the Sky

This is the final blessing chapter, made on June 24, 2025, to the music of Bryan Adams' song "Heaven," playing on Miriam's radio.

Her day began with errands and the gentle companionship of Mocha. The universe began to weave an extraordinary thread through the ordinary. This was the day that Miriam began collaborating with her chosen writer, the one who would write not just her story but that of the Animal Kingdom, Spirit, and every winged, four-legged, and wild being who walked beside her. Everything braided into one truth: we are not separate from nature or from Spirit. We are whole.

The Procession of Wings

Miriam stopped at a traffic light facing east, the direction of new beginnings. Before her were three crows: one was perched on the stoplight above her, the Guardian of Thresholds. Two more were on a rooftop facing west. These were the Ancestors, watching from the past.

As the light turned green, the two rooftop crows flew across her path, moving to the left, signaling a movement into feminine wisdom and soul memory.

Seventeen more crows rose after them, bringing the total to eighteen, a number Miriam felt pressing with meaning: transformation, destiny, a quiet coronation.

She threw kisses to the wind while Mocha watched with knowing eyes. One crow stayed still, anchoring the circulating energy flowing around her. Miriam turned left, entering the next part of her life.

At another stoplight, a few moments later, a cluster of tiny birds formed a living crown above her car. She realized that she and Mocha were sitting inside a sacred sky-temple, protected and seen. The birds moved in joyous spirals, saying in Spirit's soft language: "Yes. You are in rhythm."

All day, the messengers arrived. Butterflies fluttered around her like pages from a cosmic journal, each wing a syllable, each flight a sacred word. Yellow butterflies spoke of solar joy and personal power rising. White butterflies signified Spirit, purity, and messages from beyond. They hovered above her like scribes of the invisible.

The Song that Opened the Sky

As Miriam returned home with Mocha in the early afternoon, the sacred messages continued.

Listening to K-EARTH 101, she heard the song "Heaven" by Bryan Adams.

She was already in a state of full-hearted gratitude. The radio sang, "You're all that I need," and Miriam understood the line as addressed to the Creator, not to another person. God was all she needed. In that listening, she heard her mother's steady voice within her memory:

"It had to happen that way...

It was destined for you to awaken."

In the song, she heard this line: "It's hard to believe we're in heaven..."

She knew she was not waiting to arrive in Heaven, because she was already there.

Heaven is presence, awareness, forgiveness, and love that is returned.

Heaven is walking forward in divine truth.

Declaration of Unity

Miriam recognized this day as the sacred convergence. The crows flew because the story was ready. The birds circled because the crown had been cast.

The butterflies danced because her path was blessed.

The song played because Spirit sang with her, and her soul replied:

"I will speak, not only for myself, but for every animal, every wind, every ancestor, because we are not separate. We are One."

Let this be the closing chapter and the sacred opening.

Miriam knew that her story no longer belonged to her; it now belongs to the wild, the seen, unseen, the wings, and the whispers that walked beside her.

This was the day her story began to fly.

And So, It Was Told...

A Sacred Collaboration with the Animal Kingdom, the Wind, and the Divine

Benediction: We Give Thanks

To all who walked beside me,

In love or in silence,

In light or in shadow,

I give thanks.

To the ones who lifted me,

And to the ones who let me fall, I give thanks.

For every fall became flight,

And every sorrow carved a deeper place for the Creator to live within me.

To the animals,

who never forgot the language of Spirit,

To the wind,

Which carried messages when I could not speak,

To the feathers, the fur, the wings, and the watchers,

I give thanks.

Even the hardest moments were holy.

Even the broken places became sacred altars. They led me closer.

To the truth. To the light. To the One.

May this story be a lantern.

May it remind others that we are not separate. Not from each other.

Not from the Earth. Not from the Divine.

We are whole.

We are woven.

And we are, each of us, A whisper from Heaven.

Amen. Aho.

And so it is.

This book is not an ending; It is a beginning. Carried by wings, paws, and whispers, it travels outward, for all beings, in every realm, with love.

—

www.ingramcontent.com/pod-product-compliance
Lightning Source LLC
Chambersburg PA
CBHW051229120626
46547CB00013B/1575